Fierce Shimmer

Poems for Mama

Ellen Marie Hinchcliffe

Fierce Shimmer
Poems for Mama
From The Hive Press
Copyright 2012 by Ellen Marie Hinchcliffe

ISBN-13: 978-1475225778
Title ID: 3703747

Poems

In the secret grove of the heart
May we ever meet.

-Caitlin Matthews

Ellen Marie, Mama and the Moon   1992

In Body (Mama)

Down on the ground, bent strangely from the waist
holding Lung Wort's spotted leaves between fingers
Lucille croaks "Baby there is no mouth..."
trying to say I love you in the shape of leaves
I hope You, Lucille and Paula
Meridel, Marie and June
Gloria, Pat and Gigi
Molly, Essie Mae and Mae Birdsong too
I hope you are having a good time
pouring the wine straight from the vine
deep laughter among the violets
to be the violets and damn, ladies
while I still have a mouth
hear me trying to say, I love you
in the shape of
a poem.

After Lucille Clifton's poem Out of Body

Hekate   1997   M.K.Glover

Universe Becomes Bear

You Left Us All the Beauty

The stiff black fur
Carries you deep into black night
All is black here except for stars…
You say, throwing your dark hair back
Across your shoulders
You are visiting me again
In dreams, I never want to wake from
I struggle to stay in that warm place
Of you, I go searching for it
What is left but
The velvet black of bears fur
Cradling you in her arms
You are Mother, you are daughter
You look up
Stars flit around your face
Where you almost never saw beauty
But left it all for us
To hold tightly against our chests
And miss you.

Breaking (First poem since you died)

Memories could break me open
my own heart, against
what you suffered
again and again
I am swimming
through you,
dark ocean
searching for you

So much missing I could drown
I hear your voice rise up
in the foamy sea,
Swim girl

and I do Mama,
as waves break against me
cold shock
that life goes on

without you.

Arriving Safely (August 2008)

We drove to Cape Cod, singing loudly to Bonnie Raitt
walked across the beach
and into pine woods
shaped by wind

After hours of wandering, realized
we were completely lost
panic gave way to laughter
as we tromped over sand dunes
gave up finding the car
and sat by the ocean, watching the sunset
then suddenly, without effort
we knew the way back

I have held always the image of you, swimming out
into the Atlantic, alone at night
to release the child
who would have been my sister or brother
small circle of blood
into the salty water

You swim strong, one arm cradling
one arm pushing through dark waves
I know I was not there
but I feel myself,
anxiously waiting on land
for your safe return

It's not the cancer that hones us
it's the deep pulsing love
a knife we wield, shining off the water
like the sun,
like all that laughter
It cuts you free
and we swim together, at last
clear to the other shore.

Cancer Poem

Cancer is heavy, like suicide
like rape it pulls down the page
keeps us on the run
you say cancer and people shake their heads
ask just enough questions to reassure themselves
like rape, they want to know where she was
what she did, skirt too short maybe
not the right friends
or as someone said to me after Mama died
"Didn't you say your Mom had a lot of anger?
In Chinese medicine anger is stored in the ovaries
so that makes sense."
I wanted to slap them but I didn't, I used to do that too
protect myself with- people get cancer because
they don't let their emotions out
they do something bad, wrong, ignorant
then my beautiful, emotional mother
who ate well, lived well, laughed as often as she cried
got ovarian cancer stage four
lived three years fighting it
and then she died.

She didn't get cancer because she was angry
she got cancer because it's luck of the damn draw
because we are earth
and what is done to the earth
is done to us
the soil
the air
the water
and our own sweet mortal flesh.

Fierce

In the ER you could not breathe
they had to put in a chest tube
I told the doctor I would not leave,
If you were going to die
I was going to be there.
She saw that I meant it
She let me stay.

I held the soles of your feet in my hands
I wrapped you in multi-colored strands of energy
I never looked up as five people held you down
cut you open and you cried out in pain
I said *I'm here Mama, I'm here.*

I said, Please *don't give her morphine
her pain responds to Dilaudid.
She is opiate tolerant please give her a full dose.*
And they listened, blessed is the world
for a doctor who listens

As blood and lung fluid soaked the sheets
of the gurney
all the way to your feet
and I held on
I held the energy
I held the only part of you I could.

Then in the intensive care unit at 5am
the nurse would not listen and laid your bed flat
and you were in so much pain
he was so focused on a clean gown
and not hearing me
that you could not lie flat, that you needed pain meds
before they tried to move you
and he told me to *stay out of the way,
that his priority was to do his job*

and me shouting , *I take care of her every day,*
my priority is her so you need to listen to me!
he gave you pain medication
and left in a huff, left you in that bloody gown
until the next nurse came on duty
twenty minutes later.

When he was gone through tubes and drugs
and trauma you smiled that smile and said,
Ellen, you have no respect for authority.
I wonder where you get that?
and we laughed just a little
with the sun rising
in the narrow window.
you took my hand
Thank you for going into the jaws of hell with me.
And I said, *Anytime, Mama*
Anytime.

You were in the hospital a long time, that time
it was the last time
and you came home
and we had six weeks together
before you died.

And I want it all back
I want to go on caring for you
your fierce protector
because life without you scares me
more than blood
more than anything
we ever faced together.

That Night

That night in the hospital
they drained your lung again
with a long thin needle
and I couldn't be with you
so I sat in the empty dark
waiting room
until this man came to find me
he had carefully inserted the needle
so you could breathe
he said, your Mom is amazing
I said, I know
he said the thing with doctors is
they come at death with a baseball bat
he swung towards me
and I rooted to the spot
did not flinch
but she is going to go soon
once this starts happening
over and over the lungs filling up
and they will never say this to you
but she doesn't seem like the kind of woman
who wants to go under lights in the hospital
am I right? I said yeah, that's right
I sounded calm as if we were talking about baseball
and he was urgent as if passing on secret messages
he talked about hospice
he said falls coming she should spend it at home
get a wheel chair take some walks
maybe she dies looking at the leaves or you
instead of strangers
I hope it's okay that I am telling you this
but they won't and your Mom
she is something else, I can tell
she shouldn't die in here
I thanked him still rooted to the spot
he shook my hand
his handsome face,
his warm hand.

The Sound I Made

Driving myself home from the hospital
over the river
the bridge arching back
towards the black sky
and I

A terrifying sound
breaks through
what we have not yet spoken,
You are dying

The scream lasts
the length of the river
and then I am silent.

Ritual for Night

You would say, Okay
if I need to turn on the light?
The switch is here in arms reach
If I want to stop the music?
Push this button on top
If I need you?
I am ten feet away on the couch
If I have trouble breathing?
We will turn the oxygen up
If I need more dilaudid?
We will put it in your G-tube slowly
so you don't throw it back up
Okay?
Okay
Let me just make sure I am clear
Okay
The light
The music
You
Oxygen
Pain meds
Then you would give me a sly little smile
Now I will be good
And we would laugh
And then
Both go to sleep
Sometimes for an hour
Sometimes for two
Then we would be up again
Light
Music
Me
You
Oxygen
Pain
And sips of water

I would climb in bed with you
We would watch Arrested Development
Desk Set or Persuasion on loop
Drift in and out
Talk to or about the cat

Sometimes you would be scared
And I would comfort you
Or I would be scared
And you would say
I'm okay, love
Okay
Light
Music
Me
You
Oxygen
Pain
Sips of water
Laughter
The whirring of the pump
The arranging of the various tubes
Moving pillows
Positions
Foot rubs
And maybe
A little sleep
Mixed in between
Our long loving
Journey
Through night
To one
more
day.

Your Body

I mention to no one, not even you
the brilliant red clots that slip down your G-tube
a month ago they would have been cause for alarm
now, I marvel at the beauty of blood
the clots look like rubies

I rub your back as you lay on your side
such velvet skin, stretch marks from two babies
and 65 years of growth spread across your round hip
like the sun, like branches of the oak
I have never seen anything more beautiful
Life mapped on the body.

How We Reached for Pleasure

How we reached
how we reached
for pleasure

this woman likes good food
this woman likes good times
this woman likes good wine

How we reached
how we reached
for pleasure

Your body my landscape
your hip my hill
where I rest my head
we are climbing still

How we reached
how we reached
for pleasure

sage and rose and lavender
good smells
for the woman who
can't eat

foot rubs and back rubs
and temples anointed
good touch
for the woman who
can't breathe

How we reached
how we reached
for pleasure

How we reached
how we reached
for pleasure.

Hekate's Dogs

"The earth began to bellow, trees to dance
and howling dogs in glimmering light advance
Ere Hekate has come..."
                                    - Virgil from The Aeneid

Towards the end
You begin to see
The Black dog move through
Brush past you in the green chair
Head towards the kitchen or weave between
You and those that come to visit

You speak of the dog only to me
Her presence is a comfort, you say
It's okay that only I can see her
a question, an affirmation
Yes Mama

Only after you died
Did I realize
It was Ute, Ted's sweet Rottweiler
that died a few years back

She had arrived, your son's dog
a comforting emissary of Hekate
The goddess that always repays
being remembered
Her daughter at the three way crossroads
apple spilt open
small cakes in hand

Up through the ladder
And down again
She sent her companion

To bring you back.

The Black Dog Shows Up

The day Dr. Sandler came and sat quietly in the living
room. You sat across from him in your green chair and
I sat on the ottoman my hand touching your knee.
He asked what you wanted from this time, which made
me want to throw up but I stayed steady as you said to
make some art, spend time with family then you
faltered, maybe to get better?

You looked at me confusion on your face. I took your
hand and told Dr. Sandler it could be overwhelming.
He agreed. He was calm and really kind, he was so
helpful with pain management, which we had struggled
with for too long on our own but he didn't say, Kathy
you are dying. He didn't say death at all.

After he left, you told me, *Ellen, I keep seeing a black
dog walk through the house. I'm pretty sure no one
else is seeing it but really I don't mind it being there.*
I said, *I didn't mind either.* You smiled and then you
looked panicked, gripped my arm, *I feel dumb I think
I messed up my answers. No Mama, your answers
were great he asks too many questions.*

Later when I was making up your TPN you asked Dad,
Am I going to die? he said, *Yes. That's what I thought.*
You replied shutting your eyes.

The hospice book advises to assure people what they
are seeing isn't real. Don't indulge their hallucinations.
But the black dog kept pacing through the house, like
death itself

and who was I to say she wasn't there.

The Day Before You Left

In the snow after two days of working
like a hive, no speaking, it was hard Mama
not to talk with you
we had shared everything, always
I had not left your side for more than
a handful of minutes
not since the night you were so weak
I carried you the fifteen feet
from living room to bedroom in a wheelchair
now I took a walk by the river
I felt you so strongly among the Oaks
on that snowy path
like I had not felt you
in that small pink room in days
and I saw the big black bear
shambling away from me
holding you
in her arms over and over
you changed from a baby
to a laughing child
to a woman
she began to run with you
through the snow
I wanted to follow
I cried out and I heard you say
"Stay, you can not come
not yet. I'm okay, I'm everywhere
I'm everything."
I stood there bereft
my heart pounding
in the silence of winter

suddenly I was surrounded
by hundreds of robins
they encircled me in the trees
I sang and sang to you
I closed my eyes
I opened them
the robins remained, sturdy sentinels
then Eagle flew over head
soared off in the direction
Bear had taken you
I knew it was coming
I knew you were going
I returned to the pink room
for one last night of vigil.

Dream (Soon After)

Upended birdhouses
full of fairy tale mice
a wide green hill
you flying
a giant blue bird
with sharp wings
I stand on the ground, afraid
I call for you to be careful
Gigi stands no taller than the mice
on the branch of an evergreen
in a blue flowered dress
she looks as I knew her
great grandmother, thick ankles
sturdy shoes, white hair
but her words (and size) are magical
she can't get hurt
she's having fun
I blink at Gigi realizing
her words are true
The little people are looking after her
she assures, *I watch over her now*
the giant blue bird
my mother flying free
lands momentarily as
she was in life
a full-bodied woman
chestnut hair and a way
of smiling with her mouth closed
that took up her whole beautiful face
she takes my hands
and dances with me in a circle
round and round
she is laughing
then takes flight again
and is gone from sight.

Protection 2006   M.K. Glover

Mama, Inanna
and those kitchens talk.

Mama, Inanna and Those Kitchens Talk

"The black sky wants your ass purified..."
  - Michele T. Clinton

Mama goes down
it ain't easy
Mama, Inanna and those kitchens talk
under the stars
the house
under the house is dirt
Mama goes down
clutching this story to her breast.

Mama comes up
it ain't easy
Mama, Inanna and those kitchens talk
sputtering soil like a diver
cupping blood between hands
a bouquet of all that must be lost
to survive.

In the kitchen coffee black as night
full of women there is talk
Mama pushes heavy chestnut hair from her eyes
and laughs, "Girls, let me tell you about hell
and how I just got back."

I Am the Woman Left

I am the woman left
turning in sleepless dark
all the women before me
knotted in my hair
before me, Mama
now I am you, I say
in the simplest ways
buying the yellow potted primrose
because they smell of earth
because any color is welcome
at the end of February
I wake in my bedroom
that was your painting studio for 12 years
I wake in tired bones and rise
drink coffee
as you did, with a cat in my lap
with too much
and not enough
wrestling always
in the close tangle
of my heart.

You Loved Yourself Best

You loved yourself best
when you rode your own body
like a horse through the city
like Joan of Arc
to battle
the red eyed woman
wielding the crescent moon
a scythe
cutting the thin air before you

You loved yourself best
waves parting against strong thighs
as you dove into the Atlantic
swam out past safety
or any hope of rescue

Only then would you reappear
a smiling queen
of no man's country
your sparkling crown of salt
drying in dark hair.

Mama Wasn't Always Easy

Mama wasn't always easy
Mama called herself bitch
Mama cut the soft place of her arms, left scars
Mama said fat, ugly, stupid and unlovable
and meant only her, only her
Mama yelled, bellowed and banged about
Mama raged and shattered, ripped her face
from pictures in the family albums
Mama drove once into a telephone pole
Hoped? Dared to die?

Mama wasn't always easy
but Mama was a joy
Mama wasn't always easy
but Mama was full of love
Mama wasn't always easy
but Mama was brave, funny, warm
beautiful, talented, sweet and kind
Mama wasn't always easy
but Mama would do anything for you.

But damn, Mama wasn't always easy
Mama wasn't always easy
on herself.

In The Light (one month after)

At sunset, I get dressed up to drink and dance
in the living room, as we did so many times before
I light all the candles, arrange everything just so
change my earrings- the pink teardrops you gave me
last summer, put on more of the peony perfume you
bought for my birthday and my favorite ratty skirt
my private party skirt and
from the first song
from the first sip of cold beer
it all comes streaming through me
and I play all the songs and dance so hard, my feet
turning and sliding against the pattern of wool carpet
I sing so loudly
I laugh so wildly and I cry,
I cry like a banshee
I cry in the high place of the song
the cry becomes a chant
the chant becomes a body
of light and I am inside the light
I am the light, you are the light, all held by the cry, by
the song, by the dancing, by the joy, by the moment,
I spin and spin into it because I am your daughter and
you taught me how, because you gave me the space,
because you opened the space, because you were the
space where this could be, where I could be, you let
me be, you joined me, we always knew how to party
Mama, in the sacred sense of the word and it is the
one place I can still open and feel you completely
in the body of light
is the body
you danced into being
is your beautiful full body, sashaying to the song
is your song and here, wild eyed and screaming
laughing and crying
dancing and dancing
light streaming from me
is your only daughter
and she goes on…

On My Bad Days

On my bad days, I am full of the calculations
Why does Paul Newman get to live to 80?
Or more to the point, why you and not Dick Cheney?
The woman at the restaurant was easily 75
and laughing
You were 65 and not done.

And it was not all for the best
Not God's plan
Not the beauty of Kali's destruction
Not anything that makes any sense.

I keep thinking it was a mistake
I am waiting for the paper work to arrive
the spiritual
the contractual
or conjure moment of your return
"Oh here she is, sorry about all that."

Or I confuse your death with winter itself
when spring returns
surely you will be come back to us
Who else can tend your garden?
Who else can take your place?
How can Mama die?
How can you die?
How can you possibly not be alive?

Talons Strike

Before you can not imagine
fathom all things happen so fast
a strike of talons
only later slow and aching
in a sleepless night, comes the reality
you died of cancer

you feel stolen from me
by heavy metals in the soil
benzene in the water
spewed out from the oil refinery
Lima, Ohio where you were a girl
where the soil was carried
on the soles of your bare feet
the water parting
on your lips

something strikes fast in your cells
one day it will take you
this wrong turn, human made
your good tender body
does not realize the change
and continues to grow
unabated
towards
the sky.

Tender (three months after)

Three months since your death, passing
to the minute, I light candles through out the house
hum without realizing it
Nobody's Fault but Mine…
I remember the blue light, your bare head
the last breaths slow, a pause, great work already done
ease at the end
how can something so beautiful
also be so terrible, both nightmare and vision
both comfort and wound
I will always carry
You, your death.

Poured wine
old wine in the melting snow
new wine from the frig in the pink stemware
on your altar
tempted to join you, but it's 3:40pm
hell I think, spirits don't have use for time
marking, but I do
the wine is cold
and tastes like everything
sweet and good
sharp and womanly.

The sun emerges at the tail end of a gray day
floods the flowers on your altar
they glow from within
I sit in this pool of sun
sipping wine
for the moment
I follow memories unafraid
deer paths through birch
such tender trails
you lead me on
to rest
and safety.

Too Much

Too much coffee leaves my bowels watery
and squeezed but it's so good on the tongue
I say, pouring another cup
you understand, everything
how much I want, how deep my lust and needs
I never want anyone to leave, ever
lovers that were no good for me
and me strong and proud would beg and beg
make promises to have no needs
I never want the party to end, don't go
sleep here, in my bed, stay
lets wake late and make pancakes
and drink too much coffee
and talk and talk.

I always want to talk too much
how many times did I arrive at your door
for more coffee, more food, more wine, more talking
unraveling stories of heartbreak into fantastic tales
that made you shake your head and laugh
I loved to make you laugh
you were never too much for me, ever
and I was never too much for you.

Who now is left to shake their head
so lovingly at me? Knowing all I am
and how deeply I long to be known
how I know you that way, now even your bones.

I carry your bones and ashes
from room to room,
I cry to them
don't leave, talk to me
talk and talk
and want too much

You wanted to live, I know this
I carry this, I cradle this, your bones
and ashes, the weight comforting.
I dress them in shells and rocks,
as if getting ready for a party

And because I never want anything to end
because I want too much,
I wrap what is left, carefully
in a piece of Nana's old quilt
and hold you in my arms
like a new born.

Grief

Sometimes grief seeps from me
pools slowly in my cupped hands
Sometimes grief explodes over me
whorls of white light
knocking me to the ground.

Mostly I think for a moment
I see you in the aisle of the food co-op
and it catches in my throat,
as I step forward
so eager, just to say hello.

Alone

Somewhere I am
crashing to the ground.

I turn to find you there
you say to me
"Ellen, I did not die.
It has taken me awhile
to get back to you."
then you turn
and dive

I follow you into the green pool
swimming hard, not wanting to lose sight of you
again. But I can not keep up
and your body disappears
in the green shadows before me.

I wake suddenly to find I am not swimming at all
but flying through cold white skies
and I am alone.

Woman Dances in Front of Death   M.K. Glover

Death's Daughter

Death's Daughter

Shit I used to talk so big
Scorpio girl chatting up the ancestors
Wearing skeletons like party dresses
Carting skulls around like shiny purses
So easy with death, it was my middle name
Worn on my ring finger, like the happiest bride.

Then death took you,
The one person I couldn't live without
And suddenly I was screaming
Beating at her smooth dark surface
Give her back!
Give her back to me!

All night I look for you
In deep waters, under the moon
Talons flash
You feel stolen from me
By your own cells,
By chemicals in the blood
And no one to answer my cries
Of why?

I am death's daughter now
I always was
Out here with death and you
Alone in this little boat
Crazy, weeping, rowing
A long way back
to shore.

Death Speaks

I am not cancer
I am not a heart attack
or disease

I am not a car wreck
or a terrible fall
I am not murder
or starvation

I am not bombs
or guns
or knives

I am not old age
or stillbirth

I am death
and I weep with you
and I carry those
you love
in my arms
and deliver them
to the universe

All day long
and through the night
forever, as gently as I can
I carry the living
home

and ask only
that you remember me
a glass of whisky, poured neat
a pretty flower, tended in it's vase
a single candle, kept burning
for my weary task
for my part in all things
that must be.

Mama Left a Clue

In her apron of snakes
you loved her
you knew her
you left her for me
to stumble upon
to study
to at last open and see
yes daughter I can hear you coax
she is death
make friends with her
the universe will open then
honor her
and in this way
you honor me.

Looking at Death (For Alma Luz Villanueva)

A naked woman
belly and breasts soft and low
dances in front of
her own death

Death's momentary face
rigid grimace
skull like but still
covered with flesh

Death raises her hands
palms out, fingers curled
in what looks like protest
but is truly reverence

for the woman
who dances
at the edge
before passing over

Death a fleeting
moment between
the last breath
and stillness

Death captured in the body
held by bones and flesh
an imprint, a monument
meant to crumble
to dust, burn to ash

You can not dwell in death
there is living
and there is spirit

Death is a gateway
not a place itself
Death is a door we pass through
on our way to some place else.

Death Speaks Through the Poet (For Lucille Clifton)

I am death, she said
beautiful and terrible in my beauty
and they run from me
as if I am to blame
they will not look upon my face
with recognition
though I could comfort and soothe
if they would allow it
but no, they hide me away
and refuse to honor what they see
in that moment
arms askew,
mouth open
and skull tight
my apron of snakes
they make of me horror
when I am the sacred
doorway
to forever
when I am transformation
one of two

Birth is bloody
and beautiful and
changes everything
and so do I
so do I
so do I.

Tiny Death

The single firefly
close enough to touch
then high above the river birch
tiny ember
blinking gold
in blackness

        I am.

The bee disappears
through the tongue of the flower
heavy with pollen
magenta embrace

        I am.

The tiny brown ants
march from earth
a female mass

        I am gone.

Being
all
things
a tiny death
each time.

The Voices Arrive

The first voice
was river
after, you
and Paula
two squat blue owls
perched on my shoulders
offering
unsayable council.

Moon Rise Over Sand Dunes 2002   M. K. Glover

Return Again

Vision

Half death
half life
split down the middle
opening

A woman in a long dress
gold, blue and green
a small bird at her throat
light spilling.

Grown Up Songs

These are grown up songs, I am
Somewhere between,
My mama and the child who will come
My mama somewhere between, the dead and me

My daughter, my son, out there in the universe
Hands on hips, bigger than little planets
And me?
I stand between

Earth, my mama
The stars, my child

It's the blood that flows in all of us
I am between them

Reaching, touching,
both sides
of now
and forever.

Written for Mama after her Mother died, 1993.

Birthday Poem

Another winter day, crystal white and blue
stalagmite icicles, touch roof to ground
house is heavy with scent, forced blooms
in cold basement, now appear, a totem of spring
months early but how the heart needs coaxing
to open anew. These blooms in honor of your birthday
always I gave you purple hyacinth, in February
and always you gave to me, when my heart was weary
bundled against cold, past remembering
you were always my spring, even now
you continue to burst forth from death
and bloom.

How Spring Arrives from Death Each Year

The sound of birds
singing melts snow
dead wood
polished by ice
blooms
from what
appears gone

Shiny black crows
against blue sky
making tomorrow
possible
by keeping today
turning
towards that leap
in the chest

The moment of flight
small brown ants
appear from earth
rivers
bending towards
patient hands

Bees
thick with gold
dream worlds
to kiss flowers
in this one
and make us new
again.

On Keeping Mama's Gardens Going

Playing in the dirt
I never really knew
until I took over
for you
what it means
to tend the plants
come to know
the geography of
green
growing
the absolute leap
of faith
each time you push
a seed to soil
dare to fall in love
with color and abundance
only to watch flowers fall back
death's hollowed husks
mark
each grave
a bed
for winters silent head
then come warm breeze
you pull back
skeletons
and start again
laboring towards
the same
end
less
end.

We are Loved

Today I walked in the woods
I head Robins call
I thought, they are calling me
And my heart leapt.

My mind said sternly, in minds way, *Birds call*
but not for you. You are not chosen, it is coincidence
nothing more.

River spoke (she is stronger and quieter than mind)
The Robins call you because you are loved.

I walked on, daughter that I am
As Robins called to me
Not because I am special, chosen
But because I am beloved
Imagine that, we are all called
All of us, because we are loved.

Let Me Go To Flame (For Jennifer Shafer)

Early morning camp, cold and cloudy
the call of jays
the way it stretches, scrambles time
My fire burns hot
dancing orange flames
black tipped, a foot high

The fire
like salmon in the creek
Mama's stars yesterday in the river
Mama herself
right there in arms reach
but otherworldly

I cannot touch
fire, salmon, stars, Mama
but I can be with
be close
talk to (in a fashion)
these rocks under my feet

When I die
let me go to flame
to ash, to stars
carry me if you would
in all manner of places
to rivers, oceans, streams
to oak, pine and birch
to willow, maple and linden
nestle me in moss beds
secret me in city plants

Make circles of me in red earth
make thresholds of me
designs and patterns
of pottery, throw me
to the moon
throw me a good party and
into the wind

And after that
what is left, give back to fire
where in the dying embers
I can breathe.

December 7th

Dad said something really important, *"What happened with Mom was the hardest thing we ever went through but it was never grim. She was always so alive even when dying."*

Mama, this passing time 3:40pm
finds me puttering
a little cleaning, a little decorating
thinking, mulling, conceiving,
cursing (when the picture I am hanging is crooked)
laughing at myself for cursing (so you)
watching the birds come and go from the feeder
the cats perfecting sleep in all the best places
arranging altars
listening to the Revels
eating thoughtfully
remembering
just being
awake enough to know
in some ways, this is truly the best of life

you taught me that
gratitude
for the simple, good, daily
and for joy
when it lights on your heart
to follow it through
to that momentary place
where it all falls away
and you are the all

I took a long walk by the river
the Robins appeared
catching winter light
their orange bellies glowed
gliding over me
each one a little sun! I cried
and cried, cleansing tears
a clean sing
a song of clearing

Three years now since you breathed in blue light
and let go, three years since bear carried you
laughing over the hill
three years and not a moment has passed
that I did not miss you keenly
sometimes with great joy
sometimes with great sadness
mostly with both together

You are still my teacher, my beloved
today was nice, your kind of day
from the coffee I made us this morning
strong and sweet, to this moment

the sun now low, the shadows long
gold and blue turns soon to night
I am waiting for Dad to come over for dinner
I am breathing, living
and loving you in all of it.

Mama

I don't want to grieve you
So much as feel you
And in the garden
Watering
I am you.

Dream (For Juma)

Walking with Juma on the path
I know best
to the white pine
that holds Mama's voice
the path scattered light
brown and green
before us
a slumbering black bear
curled vast and protective
around a small cub

On this path we walk
both the beloved dead
and our child to come.

The Void (For Mama and My Child to Come)

Some circuit complete
between us Mama
all I know of perfection
was our love
always the darkness
the void
you stepped through
to blink in daylight
and I still swimming in stars
did not know my name
until you pulled me through
feisty and misshapen
with my tiny fist raised
against their metal
against their time
you loved me
I turned perfect in your arms
we turning and turning
in the ever expanding
possibility
until you stepped back
through the void
last breath, blue light
and said, No you can not follow
not yet and I stayed here
blinking cold, winter light
while bear ran with you
into universe, velvet dark
I am the one relearning
to call your name, to balance
at the edge
where the void opens
just enough for your lovely voice
to wind through

and my child
my slipstream, my wild chance
out there in the void with you
rainbow in the sacred dark
not through my body
but still I am universe
conduit
opening of mystery
where names not yet given
shimmer like rivers
even now,
I am pregnant
with all
that love.

Fierce Shimmer

Yellow in my hands
Calls me to trace terrible, beautiful stories
Spirals on the black
Bear
Universe
All is black here
This river
Backbone
Horizon
You are the land
How else to tell it?
The fierce shimmer
Steps through the void
And back again
Leaves Rivers
Backbone
Horizon
Leaves yellow cornmeal
Silver ashes
Heavy with
Falling stars
Through my hands
Incantation
to break open
as the Daughter is called
Mama
Nana
Gigi
Few things calmed you more in the end
The beehive transformation
Before me
The fox with eyes of bees (just after death)

Mama
Nana
Gigi
River
Backbone
Horizon
We are the land
The root cycle turning into view
Fierce shimmer
You
You
You.

Dance You Back

Dance the ashes
into earth
the kneading of dough
to rise
rise in green
rise up again

Ashes thrown triumphant
to the moon
fall scattered stars
a circle
anoint the ground
where seeds pushed deep
where roots and tendrils
curl towards light
and dark
anoint me

Covered I am
in you
sacred I am
for you
for dancing
with the voices
round and round
I dance
you back
I dance you back
I dance you back
to earth
to life.

Forever Song

Universe becomes bear
bear becomes me
I move full bodied

Life becomes death
death becomes free
I move weightless,
almost flying

Bones become stars
return again

Woman becomes spirit
she always was

Spirits become voices
children listen,
the universe is our home
we are home
forever

The universe is our home
we are home
forever.

From Mama and Paula translated as best I could.

This book is dedicated to my amazing Mama, M.K. Glover who went by Kathy. Grandmother, painter, teacher, gardener, feminist, avid reader, cat lover, free spirit, dancer, friend, student of the Goddess and beautiful woman who lived well, gave much and always loved a good time. Never enough words to say how much I love you, Mama. My life's work. xo

Mama painting with her cat Natasha as company.   1980

Bear, Robin, River, Snake, The Small Brown Ants,
Hekate, Spiderwoman…

and to the patient, loving voices that do not die.

The circle which is a spiral stretches
out to the Star of Isis it is the stair
of Light in the upper parts. glow

Spring

the Grandmothers laughing
The Ancestress reaches her hand
to draw us up. She is a white vulture
with a spiral neck our flesh flickers
& changes like flame. Like flame it holds us
fast.

A page from Mama's artist journal.

With Gratitude and Affection-

Honoring Paula Gunn Allen for her books, bold thinking and sweet hospitality. Lucille Clifton for her stunning poetry, especially her writing of the voices. Meridel LeSueur for writing so big of the body/ land and for her line, The Root Cycle Turning into view.

John Trudell for his clarity and his crazy. His willingness to share both keeps me alive. Please listen to him.

Paula's daughter, Lauralee Brown for sharing with me the daughter's path.

Sharon Day and Louis Alemayehu for much inspiration.

Alma Luz Villanueva, Mama's favorite poet. Her poem Grandmother's Song I read aloud to Mama the last night before she passed over. I am blessed by her generosity as a poet and the path she blazes for passion and justice.

Rachel Moritz for invaluable editing provided while working, being a poet and the Mother of a toddler.

Ayanna Muata for her photography and Scorpio heart.

Gretchen Erickson, Karen Woodson, Jennifer Shafer, Rocklynn Culp, Kristin Rasmussen, Rebecca Pearcy, Moe Lionel and Chris Sherman.

My beautiful father, Richard Hinchcliffe. Eleanor and Henry Erickson Hinchcliffe for being my greatest joy.

My brother Ted, for the gift of your children, for your astounding generosity, humor and love of celebration that does Mama proud and for all your cancer research.

Gabrielle Francine Civil for all our art days, wine nights and for pulling from the hive so much creative energy.

Juma B. Essie my husband and long time companion for the root and joy that is our daily life, for your wicked sense of humor and for seeing me whole against the sky. xo

Contact- fierceshimmer@gmail.com
Website- http://sites.google.com/site/ellenhinch/

Fierce Shimmer is available through Amazon or if
possible please consider ordering copies through a local
bookstore.

From the Hive Press is the creative collaboration of
Ellen Marie Hinchcliffe and Gabrielle Francine Civil.

Cover design by Ellen Marie Hinchcliffe
Photography of Ellen on cover by Ayanna Muata
http://web.me.com/ayanna.muata/Waning_Moon_Digital_Images

All paintings and drawings are from M.K. Glover's
remarkable body of work.

Ellen Marie Hinchcliffe is a poet, performer, videomaker, loving Daughter and Auntie. She was born on Dia de los Muertos in Dayton, Ohio 1968 and named for both her Grandmothers. She is of English, Irish and German decent.

Her performance work includes, "Dirty the Bones- on being white and other lies..." She is currently working on a documentary film about the late, great writer/thinker Paula Gunn Allen. Her video short, Art Letter premiered on Twin Cities Public Television in 2010.

Ellen lives with Juma B. Essie and three fabulous cats two blocks from the Mississippi River in Minneapolis, Minnesota. Together they are beginning the journey towards domestic infant adoption. She is sustained by the good company of many, the gardens started by her Mama and by the occasional all night dance party. Ellen has published many poetry zines over the years and this is her first full-length book.

Chemicals dumped into our air, water, soil and food have made cancer an epidemic. Please learn the early warnings signs of ovarian cancer, as it is very difficult to detect. We are quite simply earth. What is done to earth is done to our bodies. There are many incredible organization working to stop the madness of greed-fueled pollution, please support them. I deeply respect the work of Sharon Day and all the Anishinawbe Grandmothers that started the *Mother Earth Water Walks*. I will donate a dollar to them for every book I sell. http://motherearthwaterwalk.com/

Thank you for reading these poems.

Made in the USA
Charleston, SC
21 May 2012